Daily Problems
and
Weekly Puzzlers

grade
7

mon tues wed th

2 3 4

9 10 11

by
Robert Callahan

16 17 18

Ideal

Daily Problems & Weekly Puzzlers

GRADE 7

Robert Callahan is a teacher, curriculum developer, and writer. During his eleven-year career, he has taught at many grade levels, ranging from preschool to college; and his students have included those in gifted and talented programs as well as those classified as special education students. Much of Robert's training and inspiration to write curriculum projects comes from his participation in the California Writing Project and the California Math Project. He also worked as a member of the Beyond Activities Project team for three years.

Robert holds bachelor of arts degrees in English and Psychology, as well as a master's degree in Special Education from California State University, Chico.

Cover Design: Annelise Palouda

Text Designer: Violeta Diaz

Art Director: Nancy Tseng

Illustrator: Art Glazer

Electronic Production: Joseph Parenteau

Production Coordinator: Theresa Tomlin

Editor: Sandra Riggs

Project Manager: Judy Goodnow

©1996 Ideal School Supply Company
Alsip, Illinois 60482
Printed in U.S.A.
ISBN: 1-56451-199-5
1 2 3 4 5 6 7 8 9 10 . 9 8 7 6 5

Table of Contents

Introduction

▼▼▼▼▼▼▼▼▼

This book is one of a series of six books for grade 3 through grade 8. These books provide a treasury of challenging and engaging problems from all areas of the math curriculum. The Daily Problems and Weekly Puzzlers are each keyed to the appropriate NCTM Standards, and many of them are designed for "hands-on" problem solving with common classroom manipulatives.

It is a fundamental assertion of the National Council of Teachers of Mathematics (NCTM) that the teaching of mathematics must meet the changing needs of our society. In order to achieve NCTM's goals for becoming more mathematically literate and for developing their mathematical power, this book helps students:

- Learn to value mathematics
- Become confident in their own ability to do mathematics
- Become a mathematical problem solver
- Learn to communicate, using the language of mathematics
- Learn to reason mathematically

Students entering the work force in the 21st century will need to have had much practice with thinking and processing information in different ways. Being involved in problem-solving activities helps students develop useful approaches, strategies, techniques, methods, and patterns related to thinking.

Each book contains 144 Daily Problems and 36 Weekly Puzzlers. The Daily Problems are presented four per page, and are designed to take students about 15 minutes to solve. The Weekly Puzzlers, which are presented two per page, are more complex problems designed to engage students over a longer period of time and to help them develop a variety of problem-solving strategies. Sample solutions are provided for the problems, many of which have multiple solutions. The charts on page vi indicate how all of the problems and puzzlers relate to each NCTM Standard and which problems use manipulatives.

Suggestions for Classroom Use

The problems and puzzlers are written for grade 7, but because ability levels of students vary greatly, you may need to modify the problems to meet the individual needs of your students. For example, you could have your "struggling" students do portions of whole problems or do them with a partner. You might require your advanced students to provide more detailed explanations, or to extend the problems and puzzlers in different ways.

Only one NCTM Standard is referenced for each of the 144 Daily Problems and 36 Weekly Puzzlers. However, you will find that many problems are related to more than one Standard. You can refer to these Standards to help you decide how to use these problems and puzzlers. You may want to focus on one Standard for a week or a month, or you may want to expose students to a variety of Standards over a set period of time. The cross-reference chart for the Standards is designed so that you can choose the problems and puzzlers you want. The cross-reference chart for the manipulatives is designed to show you which problems use manipulatives.

These problems and puzzlers may be given to individual students, pairs of students, or small groups. When problem solving, using partners or small-group contexts provides an opportunity for students to share their thinking verbally. Students often are better able to express their thinking in writing after they've had ample opportunities to express their thoughts verbally. Talking about problems with others helps students articulate, clarify, and modify their ideas.

Many of the Weekly Puzzlers and some of the Daily Problems ask students to extend the ideas by creating their own problems. When students have the opportunity to play with operations, algorithms, and numbers, and to create their own problems, they understand the concepts more deeply and personally. When they are involved in this way, they are constructing their own meaning as they undertake this creative process.

Hints for Using Problems and Puzzlers

- Use as an early morning warm-up. Put one or more problems on the overhead projector or chalkboard to start your day. Then have "student teacher" volunteers explain their answers to the class.

- Use as homework. Give students a Daily Problem to do each night or a Weekly Puzzler to work on all week.

- Use as a math-lab activity. Have teams work on the same problem during a math-lab period. Then have students take turns explaining solutions to the class. Or you can have student groups work on different problems and rotate the problems as they finish.

- Use in a speed contest. Have a race to see who (or which team) can solve a Daily Problem or Weekly Puzzler the fastest.

- Use in an explanation contest (the opposite of a speed contest). Have an "anti-race" to see who (or which group) can best produce a clear and detailed written explanation of a problem or puzzler with no time limit.

- Use as a transformational activity. Have students turn Daily Problems into Weekly Puzzlers, and Weekly Puzzlers into long-term investigations and explorations.

- Use as a quiz. Compile student-created problems into a quiz for everyone to do. Then correct the quiz together as a class so that students can read, answer, and explain their own problems.

- Use as a part of a student's portfolio. Have students select sample Daily Problems and/or Weekly Puzzlers to put in their portfolios and write about why they chose these problems.

Materials Needed

Many of the problems call for the use of manipulatives. We have tried to choose manipulatives that most teachers might have in their classroom.

Some of the problems specifically call for students to use a calculator. It would be helpful if calculators were available for most of the problems. In many cases, students are asked to make estimations first, and then check their estimations with a calculator.

NCTM Standards recommend that "...calculators should be available to all students at all times." The Standards go on to say, "Contrary to the fears of many, the availability of calculators and computers has expanded students' capability of performing calculations. There is no evidence to suggest that the availability of calculators makes students dependent on them for simple calculations."

Getting Started

Work through a few daily and weekly problems with your class before having students work independently or in groups. Help students work through a problem, using a problem-solving process such as the following: (1) FIND OUT what the problem means and what question you must answer to solve it; (2) CHOOSE A STRATEGY that will help solve the problem; (3) SOLVE IT using the strategy selected; (4) LOOK BACK or reread the problem and check your solution to see that it meets the conditions stated in the problem.

Model both effective and ineffective problem-solving methods when working with your class as a whole. Also model exemplary and incomplete written explanations, as well as productive and unproductive communication in groups. In this way, you will demonstrate and clarify your expectations for students in either individual or collective problem-solving situations.

Show students how to help each other. Emphasize that giving answers to a partner does not help either student to understand the concepts involved. You can make a game out of this by having students role-play appropriate and inappropriate ways of interacting with a partner and in a group.

Wrapping Up

Discuss the problems as a class after students complete them. Involve students in the discussion by having them share various problem-solving methods and strategies—allowing everyone to acquire new problem-solving tools. During discussions it is important to emphasize that many problems in math (and life) have multiple solutions. Seeing a variety of answers to a problem, and hearing how other students reached these different conclusions, underscores the need for students to remain open to more than one path or solution.

Cross-Reference Charts

NCTM Standard	Daily Problem Number	Weekly Puzzler Number
Algebra	2, 7, 12, 15, 18, 23, 27, 37, 104, 112, 114, 120, 125, 129, 134, 144	15, 21, 27, 32
Computation & Estimation	1, 6, 19, 21, 28, 30, 33, 40, 43, 45, 49, 53, 57, 61, 65	3, 17, 24, 36
Geometry	5, 22, 31, 35, 41, 48, 50, 75, 83, 99, 107, 115, 121, 127, 140	9, 19, 29, 31
Logical Reasoning	34, 44, 46, 56, 58, 63, 67, 71, 76, 78, 88, 91, 96, 105, 124	6, 8, 10, 11
Measurement	11, 13, 17, 26, 42, 54, 62, 72, 77, 87, 94, 102, 131, 133, 139, 143	1, 7, 13, 16, 25
Numbers	9, 14, 32, 66, 69, 73, 79, 82, 85, 89, 93, 97, 101, 106, 111, 113, 118, 122, 128	14,18, 33, 35
Patterns and Functions	4,20, 29, 36, 39, 51, 59, 68, 70, 80, 90, 103, 116, 130, 136,138	4, 23, 26, 30
Probability	3, 8, 10, 25, 52, 55, 60, 81, 95, 98, 110, 119, 132, 135, 137, 141	5, 12, 22, 28
Statistics	16, 24, 38, 47, 64, 74, 84, 86, 92, 100, 108, 109, 117, 123, 126, 142	2, 20 , 34

Manipulative	Daily Problem Number	Weekly Puzzler Number
Calculators	1, 4, 7, 9, 11, 14, 16, 18, 19, 21, 27, 29, 33, 35, 36, 37, 40, 42, 43, 47, 49, 54, 57, 58 61, 64, 65, 66, 68, 69, 70, 72, 73, 82, 85, 86, 89, 94, 106, 111, 113, 114, 116, 117, 118, 120, 122, 123, 126, 128, 134, 136, 138, 142,	3, 4, 7, 9, 12, 13, 14, 16, 17, 18, 20, 21, 24, 26, 30, 31, 33
Coins	8	8, 23 27
Color Tiles	20, 55, 59. 139,	11
Dice		22
Geoboards (11 × 11 pin)	5, 15, 31, 35, 143	1, 9
Linking Cubes	41, 48	
Pentominoes	2, 13, 99	
Protractors	17, 26	
Spinner		28
Tangrams	50, 75, 102	
Toothpicks	107, 127	

Daily Problems and Weekly Puzzlers, Grade 7 © Ideal School Supply Company

Solutions

DAILY PROBLEM SOLUTIONS

These are sample solutions. Many problems may have multiple answers.

DP 1: 44

DP 2: They are moving apart at 2×60 mph $= 120$ mph or two miles per minute. Distance apart (d) is given by this equation: d = 2 miles/minute × 7 minutes = 14 miles.

DP 3: Bag 1 gives the higher probability of winning: $\frac{2}{5}$ vs. $\frac{1}{3}$.

DP 4: On day 11 he covers $\frac{1}{2048}$ meter for a total distance of $\frac{2047}{2048}$ meter and on day 12 he covers $\frac{1}{4096}$ meter for a total of $\frac{4095}{4096}$ meter.

DP 5: They are: trapezoid,rectangle, parallelogram. The shapes are all quadrilaterals, they have at least two parallel sides, they have at least two sides that are of equal length.

DP 6: Solutions will vary, but possibilities include: $3 \div 3 = 1$, $3 \div 3 + 3 \div 3 = 2$, $3 \times 3 \div 3 = 3$, $3 \times 3 \div 3 + 3 \div 3 = 4$, $3 + 3 - 3 \div 3 = 5$, $3 + 3 = 6$, $3 + 3 + 3 \div 3 = 7$, $3 \times 3 - 3 \div 3 = 8$, $3 \times 3 = 9$, $3 \times 3 + 3 \div 3 = 10$.

DP 7: The price of each pizza is $13.50 + (*n* × $1.21) where *n* is the number of toppings on each pizza.

DP 8: The probability of Heads/Heads is $\frac{1}{4}$; the probability of Tails/Tails is $\frac{1}{4}$; the probability of Heads/Tails is $\frac{1}{2}$.

Sample spinner:

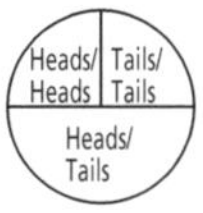

DP 9: 105

DP 10: 15 combinations

DP 11: Imagine cutting a piece $\frac{1}{2}$ km × $\frac{1}{2}$ km and moving it down. Then you can see that the Greenville field is one square kilometer in area. One kilometer = 1,000 meters, so the area is 1,000 meter × 1,000 meters or 1,000,000 square meters.

DP 12: The number of hours in the portions of the day can be found using this formula: $24 = h + 3h$; $24 = 4h$; $h = 6$. Jake was up at 6:00 AM which should be early enough to go fishing.

DP 13: Eleven pentominoe shapes have a perimeter of 12. The other has a perimeter of 10.The area for all shapes is five squares.

DP 14: Sample solution: $100 = 36 + 64$

DP 15: The point of intersection for the two equations is 1,2.

DP 16: The mean life for Brand X is 7.17 hours compared to 6.17 hours for Brand Y. The mode for Brand X is 8 hours compared to a mode of 6 hours for Brand Y. These two statistics indicate that Brand X is usually the better battery.

DP 17: The angles formed between the minute and hour hand at each hour are: 1: 30°, 2: 60°, 3: 90°, 4: 120°, 5: 150°, 6: 180°, 7: 210°, 8: 240°, 9: 270°, 10: 300°, 11: 330° and 12: 360°. Some students may argue that the angle formed at 7 (and any of the other times) can be measured in the counter clockwise direction. If this is the case, then the angle for 7 o'clock is 150° (or 360°−210°).

DP 18: The train is 1950 feet long. In twenty-six seconds, the train travels 2,600 feet. The last 650 feet of the trip do not count as part of the length of the train—the last car is merely traveling from the starting point to the end of the tunnel. Therefore the train measures its length in 19.5 seconds. $L = 19.5 \times 100 = 1950$ feet.

DP 19: One half-dollar, one quarter, two dimes, no nickels, and four pennies

DP 20: 5 years

DP 21: Since she got 25, the number she started with had to be $^{-}15.67$ times greater or $^{-}391.75$. Since she was supposed to multiply this number times 15.67, the correct answer is: $^{-}6138.7225$

DP 22: 72 square centimeters

DP 23: Youngest = $15; next = $45; next = $90; oldest = $120; total = $270

DP 24: 12

DP 25: A spinner that fits all of the clues is pictured:

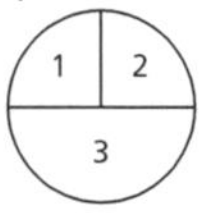

DP 26: When the hour hand is pointing directly at the three, the seconds hand makes a 76° angle with it at 3 seconds after the hour and at 27 seconds after the hour. Each second is equal to $\frac{1}{60}$ of the circle or 6° so an angle of 72° is made when it is twelve seconds before and after the hour mark for 3.

DP 27: The formula for temperature is: $t = \frac{chirps}{4} + 40$. Since we know the temperature is 84° we can solve for *c*: $84° = \frac{c}{4} + 40$; $44 = \frac{c}{4}$; $44 \times 4 = c$; $176 = c$.

DP 28: Max is 16 since $16 - 7 = 9$; $9 \times 7 = 63$ and $16 - 9 = 7$; $7 \times 9 = 63$. A simple way to solve this problem is to add the two digits $7 + 9$ to get his age. You can also solve it algebraically: $7 \times (^{-}9) = 9 \times (^{-}7)$.

DP 29: It will take eleven years for 2,000 trout to inhabit the lake. Students could solve this problem by creating a table that goes 2, 4, 8, 16, 32, 64, 128, 256, 512, 1024, 2048. They may also solve it using exponents—$2^{11} = 2048$.

DP 30: 12 guilders

DP 31: The reflections turn the top shape into a five-pointed star and the bottom shape into a letter M. The coordinates for the star are: 2,7; 0,6; 1,8; 0.9; 2,10; 3,9; 4,9; 3,8; 4,6. The coordinates for the M are: 5,3; 3,4; 3,1; 2,1; 2,6; 5,4; 8,6; 8,1; 7,1; 7,4.

DP 32: 193

DP 33: 10,000 minutes or 166 hours and 40 minutes or 6 days, 22 hours, and 40 minutes

DP 34: Path A

DP 35: The largest octagon one can make on a geoboard looks like this:

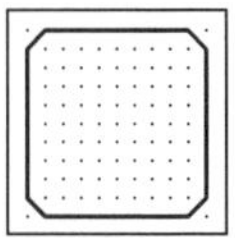

$\frac{2}{100}$ or $\frac{1}{50}$ of the geoboard is outside of the octagon.

DP 36: Yes. It will take the balloon four hours to reach the flat land. In that time it will lose 800 feet of altitude, and will have 35 feet to spare.

DP 37: At her current rate of speed, Leona finishes the course in seven hours ($t = 175 \div 25$). If she increased her speed to finish in six hours, her speed would have to increase too: $s = 175 \div 6 = 29\frac{1}{6}$ mph. This increase $= 29\frac{1}{6} - 25 = 4\frac{1}{6}$ mph.

DP 38: If the trend continues, she will be spending $45 per month at age 15 and $135 per month at age 17. The graph should look something like this:

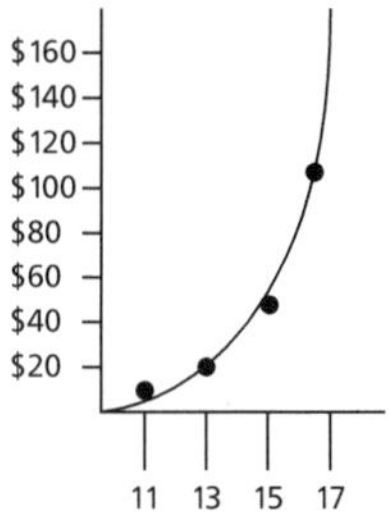

DP 39:

sides = 4, diagonals = 2; sides = 5, diagonals = 5; sides = 6, diagonals = 9, sides = 7, diagonals = 14; sides = 8, diagonals = 20; sides = 9, diagonals = 27; sides = 10, diagonals = 35; sides = 11, diagonals = 44

DP 40: $\frac{15}{16}$ of the number is 480. $480 \div 15 = 32$. $32 \times 16 = 512$.

DP 41: The shape looks like this:

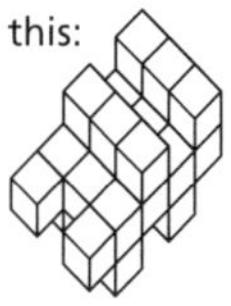

DP 42: A cake pan 20 × 24 inches has an area of 480 square inches which is four times the area of the original pan.

DP 43: Seventeen students went; they paid $23 per ticket.

DP 44: The players are seated this way:

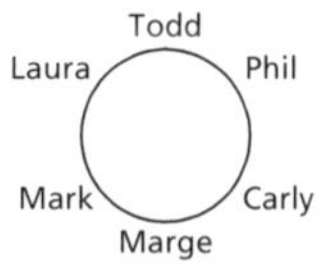

DP 45: Each subtraction results in a difference of 0.1. There are eight such subtractions plus an additional 0.1 so the expression is equal to 0.9.

DP 46: The time will be 3:05.

DP 47: Since the average score for the games is 76 points, the total points for all four games can be found by multiplying $76 \times 4 = 304$ points. The three known games total 222 points = $86 + 64 + 72$. The score for the remaining game can be found by subtracting: $304 - 222 = 82$ points.

DP 48: The linking cubes can be arranged this way:

Bottom

Green	Blue
Green	Red

Top

Red	Yellow
Yellow	Blue

(Other solutions are possible).

DP 49: All of the expressions. When you discuss this problem with the students encourage them to look at the relationships between the quotients and dividends.

DP 50: The two large triangles in a set of tangrams are congruent, so are the two small triangles. All of the triangles in a set of tangrams are similar. They are all isosceles right triangles.

DP 51: The next three numbers are: 74, 81, 162. The rule is × 2, + 7.

DP 52: Yes, the game is fair. Each player has a $\frac{13}{31}$ chance of scoring a point when a numbered square is hit.

DP 53: The correct order for the pieces starting with the one on the bottom is: $\frac{2}{7}$ $\frac{1}{3}$ $\frac{5}{11}$ $\frac{2}{5}$ $\frac{5}{8}$.

DP 54: There are two solutions: they could divide it into two pieces one 10 cm × 12 cm × 4 cm and the other 5 cm × 12 cm × 4 cm; or they could cut one piece 15 cm × 8 cm × 4 cm and the other 15 cm × 4 cm × 4 cm.

DP 55: The first draw determines which color is to be matched. After the first draw, two of the remaining five tiles match the first, so the probability of a match is $\frac{2}{5}$. This is not a fair game, even though there is an even number of each color of tile.

DP 56: The next palindrome on the odometer will be 22022—which will happen in 110 miles.

DP 57: $\frac{1}{2} + \frac{1}{6} - \frac{1}{8} - \frac{2}{3} + \frac{1}{4} + \frac{4}{9} + \frac{3}{8} + \frac{1}{18} = 1$

DP 58: Only one pair works: 16 × 625. A good way to solve this problem is by factoring: 10,000 = 10⁴ = 2⁴ × 5⁴ = 16 × 625.

DP 59:

Term	Number of Tiles
1	1
2	4
3	9
4	16
5	25
6	36
7	49
8	64
9	81
10	100

DP 60: There are 24 possible arrangements.

DP 61: .1 ÷ .5 × .6 ÷ .12 ÷ .2 ÷ .25 × .5 × .1 = 1

DP 62: Joel can get 20 rectangles or 20 sets per sheet of cardboard. Other arrangements lead to greater waste.

DP 63: Eight squares are the most that can be filled in any one game by one player. The highest score a player could get is 8 points.

DP 64: With 8 hits in 32 times at bat, Susan has a 0.250 batting average. If she gets at least three hits in the last game, she will be batting 0.306.

DP 65: Total distance traveled is given by this equation: 1,650 = 3 × h × 55; $\frac{1,650}{3}$ = 55 h; 550 = 55 h; $\frac{550}{55}$ = h; 10 = h. The family is in the car ten hours a day.

DP 66: All of the numbers are divisible by 9 and the sum of their digits is 9. The single-digit number is 9; the five-digit numbers will vary (for example 11115.)

DP 67:

DP 68: The frog that jumps 7 cm every 2 seconds.

DP 69: All perfect squares have an odd number of factors: 1, 4, 9, 16, 25, 36, 49, 64, 81.

DP 70: The other numbers are $\frac{1}{16}$, $\frac{3}{16}$, $\frac{9}{16}$, $\frac{27}{16}$, $\frac{81}{16}$, $\frac{243}{16}$, $\frac{729}{16}$.

DP 71: Divide the property this way:

DP 72: The volume of the tank can be found by multiplying 25 cm × 25 cm × 50 cm = 31,250 cm³. They can get 31 fish.

DP 73: 0, 3, 6, or 9

DP 74: The chart will be a straight line running from 0.5 cm on day one to 1.75 cm on day 5. Reading off the values for the missing data gives: Day 2 = 75 cm; Day 3 = 1.00 cm, Day 4 = 1.50 cm.

DP 75: The hexagon has four lines of symmetry. Possible solution:

DP 76: Fran is correct at 115 jelly beans, making Frankie off by 12 and Flo off by 17.

DP 77: The data is as follows

Square	Perimeter	Area
A	4 cm	1 cm²
B	7 cm	4 cm²
C	12 cm	9 cm²
D	20 cm	25 cm²
E	32 cm	64 cm²
F	52 cm	169 cm²

You may recognize that the lengths of the sides are the Fibonacci numbers.

DP 78: The numbers on each part of the clock face sum to 39 if you divide the clock this way:

DP 79: The election could take place on Nov. 2 – 8, no other days.

DP 80: 18

DP 81: The prime numbers less than 50 are: 2, 3, 5, 7, 11, 13, 17, 19, 23, 29, 31, 37, 41 ,43, 47. Since there are 15 prime numbers out of 50 numbers, the probability is $\frac{15}{50}$ or $\frac{3}{10}$.

DP 82: All of the numbers are multiples of seven. Since 100 is not a multiple of seven, these numbers cannot be used to make a sum equal to 100.

DP 83: 24 cm

DP 84: Range = 16 – 33; mode = 23

DP 85: Possible combinations include: 246 264 462 426 642 624. All of these numbers are divisible by 2, 3, and 6.

DP 86: For $\frac{2}{3}$ of the course Sam will ride 12 miles per hour. For $\frac{1}{3}$ of the course he will ride 24 miles per hour. His average speed is $\frac{(12+12+24)}{3}$ or 16 miles per hour.

DP 87: Area = 15.57 square inches; perimeter = 18 inches

DP 88: Fill the 2-liter jug from the 5-liter jug. Dump the water from the 2-liter jug into the 3.5- liter jug. Fill the 2-liter jug from the 5-liter jug. Use the water from the 2-liter jug to top off the 3.5-liter jug. There is now 0.5 in the 2- liter jug. Pour the contents of the 3.5-liter jug into the 5-liter jug which now holds 4.5 liters. Pour the water from the 2-liter jug into the 3.5-liter jug which now holds 0.5 liters. Pour two liters of water from the 5-liter jug into the 2-liter lug. The 5-liter jug now holds 2.5 liters. Pour the water from the 2-liter jug into the 3.5-liter jug. It now holds 2.5 liters.

DP 89: Two numbers less than 100 have 12 factors: 72 (1, 2, 3, 4, 6, 8, 9, 12, 18, 24 ,36, 72) and 96 (1, 2, 3, 4, 6, 8, 12, 16, 24, 32, 48, 96).

DP 90: One cut = 2 pieces, two cuts = 4 pieces, three cuts = 7 pieces, four cuts = 11 pieces, five cuts = 16 pieces, six cuts = 22 pieces. The pattern runs 2+3+4+5+6...

DP 91: Front row: Bart, Mindy, Hank, Sue; back row: Lucy, Charles, Sam, Alice

DP 92: 60% tried Extreme Chocolate, 30% tried Beyond Best Chocolate Crunch, 10% tried Vanilla Extra

DP 93: There are two pairs of numbers that fit the clues: -6,2 or 6,-2.

DP 94: The area of the smaller round tables is π × 18² = 1017.9 square inches. The area of the larger round tables is π × 21² =1385.4 square inches. Three people sit at the smaller tables so each person gets 339.3 square inches of space; four people sit at the larger tables so each person gets 346.35 square inches—the bigger tables provide the most area per person. If students measure circumference, the small tables will give more space at the edge of the table, 18.8 inches vs. 16.5 inches for the large tables.

DP 95: In one round 5 + 4 + 3 + 2 + 1 = 15 games are played. In two rounds 30 games are played.

DP 96: Since Jean is neither the youngest (and therefore not the swimmer), nor the softball player, she must play soccer. Francis doesn't have a brother and can't be the softball player so she must be the swimmer. Peg is left being the softball player.

	Softball	Swimming	Soccer
Francis	N	Y	N
Jean	N	N	Y
Peg	Y	N	N

DP 97: There are many possible pairs of integers, but they must be opposites (for instance, 6 and -6 or 15 and -15).

DP 98: The spinner looks like this:

DP 99: There are more than 2,000 different solutions. Here's one:

DP 100: The difference in prices is about $\frac{2}{3}$ or 67%.

DP 101: Examples are: 9, 25, 49, 121, 169, 289. All of these numbers are the square of a prime number.

DP 102: F,D = 0.5 square unit; G,E = 1 square unit; B,C = 2 square units; total = 8 square units

DP 103: The next three numbers are 21, 28, 36. Each number is the consecutive sum of the whole numbers starting with 1.

DP 104: 6 pm; 40 miles from camp; Rosa 2 miles ahead

DP 105: The cube is painted this way:

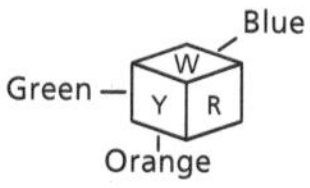

DP 106: For 3: 0, .333333, .66666; For 4: 0, .25, .5, .75; For 5: 0, .2, .4, .6, .8; For 6: 0, .16666666, .3333333, .5, .666666, .833333; For 7: 0, .1428571, .2857143, .428885714, .5714286, .8571429; For 8: 0, .125, .25, .375, .5, .625, .75; For 9: 0, .1111111, .222222222; .3333333, .44444444, .55555555, .66666666, .777777777, .88888888

DP 107: Rearrange the six internal toothpicks like this:

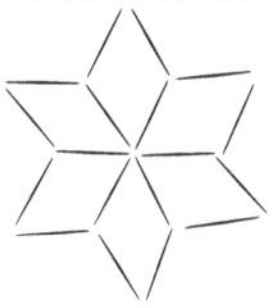

DP 108: The object picks up an additional 32 feet per second of speed for every second it falls. At the end of four seconds: 128 feet per second. At the end of five seconds: 160 feet per second.

DP 109: Yes, his method works. It is equivalent to adding up the lengths of the wood and dividing by the number of pieces (four).

DP 110: The spinner looks like this:

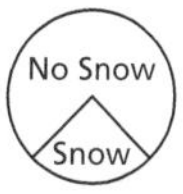

DP 111: The smallest product can be produced by multiplying 357 × 46.

DP 112: Bill has four $10 bills, six $5 bills, ten $1 bills in his wallet.

DP 113: The largest quotient is produced by dividing 987 by 56.

DP 114: Speed = mach × 760 miles per hour. Since the Shuttle orbits the earth at Mach 25 its speed = 25 × 760 miles per hour = 19,000 miles per hour. Time = 25,000 ÷ 9,000 = 1.3 hours or about one hour and eighteen minutes.

DP 115: These pairs of shapes will be on opposite sides of the cube: the circle and the heart, the square and the star, the arrow and the triangle.

DP 116: When you are eleven years old your aunt will give you $590.49.

DP 117: The mode is 38°. The mean is 40°.

DP 118: 324

DP 119: The probability is $\frac{3}{4}$ that the next fish will be a tetra.

DP 120: The formula for the years in which Halleys comet is visible is: $v = 1682 + (n \times 76)$ where n is an integer. If $n = 0$, $v = 1682$; if $n = 1$, $v = 1758$; if $n = 2$, $v = 1834$; if $n = 3$, $v = 1910$; if $n = 4$, $v = 1986$; if $n = 5$, $v = 2062$. Halley's comet was or will be visible during the lifetime of most people at least once.

DP 121: This chart represents the number of faces painted on the 27 small cubes:

Number of Faces Painted	Number of Cubes
0	1
1	6
2	12
3	8

DP 122: Goldbach conjectured that all even numbers greater than two can be written as the sum of two prime numbers. 6 = 3 + 3, 8 = 3 + 5, 10 = 5 + 5, 12 = 7 + 5, 14 = 7 + 7, 16 = 11 + 5, 18 = 7 + 11, 20 = 13 + 7, 22 = 11 + 11, 24 = 17 + 7, 26 = 13 + 13, 28 = 17 + 11, 30 = 23 + 7. Other solutions are possible.

DP 123: The sale price is 20% off. The sale price for items regularly priced $20 = $16; $25 = $20. An item with a $40 sale price is regularly priced at $50.

DP 124: At the start all three valves are closed. Step 1: Open valve 1. Step 2: Open valve 2. Step 3: Close valve 1. Step 4: Open valve 3. Step 5: Open valve 1.

DP 125: Let the speed of the boat = s. Then the upstream speed is $(s - 4)$ and the downstream speed is $s + 4$. The trip is $3 \times (s - 4) = 2 \times (s + 4)$; $3s - 12 = 2x + 8$; $s = 20$ miles per hour on calm water.

DP 126: 51

DP 127: Remove the toothpick that is at the midpoint of each side:

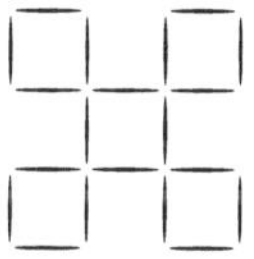

DP 128: The prime factorization of 18 = 2 × 3 × 3. To make 18 a perfect cube, you would have to multiply by two more 2's and one more 3—$2 \times 2 \times 2 \times 3 \times 3 \times 3 = 6^3$ or 216, so 12 × 18 = 216.

DP 129: Use this formula:
$a + 9 = 4 \times a$, $9 = 3 \times a$, $3 = a$.

DP 130: 270 times, 5 × 6 × 3

DP 131: 3 meters tall, 5 metric tons, 10 milliliters of medicine, 15 liters of water, 20 kilograms of hay, weighs 5 grams, travels about 2 kilometers

DP 132: Four

DP 133: The angle for each wedge measures 40°. Four pieces equal 160° or $\frac{4}{9}$ of the whole pizza.

DP 134: Answers will vary but students will be surprised to find that their hearts pump several liters of blood per minute. You can figure that the entire blood supply of the body is circulated once every minute!

DP 135: The area of the large, outer box is 4 × 4 = 16 square inches. The area of the small inner box is 2 × 2 = 4 square inches. The target space for the outer box = total outer area − inner area or 12 square inches. Probability is $\frac{12}{16}$, compared to $\frac{4}{16}$, so $\frac{3}{4}$ of the marbles should go in the outer box.

DP 136: With a 50% mark down, Aaron paid $25 for his coat. After the 30% mark down, Darrin's coat cost $35. At the cash register they took 20% off this price, so Darrin paid $28 for his coat.

DP 137: The left hand slashes show the 80% chance of making the first free throw. The right hand slashes show the 80% chance of making the second free throw. The squares with the x's in them show the chances of making both shots. There are 64 such squares, meaning that Lenny has a 64% chance of making both shots (or 80% of 80%).

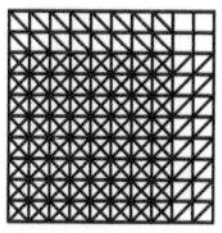

DP 138: Stop 6

DP 139: The measurements for the rectangles are: 1 × 7, 2 × 6, 3 × 5 and 4 × 4. The areas are 7 squares, 12 square units, 15 square units, and 16 square units.

DP 140: There are 23 different triangles in the figure—13 equilateral triangles and 10 right triangles.

DP 141: There are 4 pennies, 3 quarters, 2 nickels and 1 dime in the stack. The probability of picking a penny is $\frac{4}{10}$ or $\frac{2}{5}$; a quarter is $\frac{3}{10}$; a nickel is $\frac{2}{10}$ or $\frac{1}{5}$; a dime $\frac{1}{10}$.

DP 142: The temperature changed the most on January 16. It changed the least.on January. 17. The average temperature for 11 A.M. is 8.57°; The average temperature for 11 P.M. is 0.14°

DP 143: Triangle 1 = 3 square units, triangle 2 = 2.5 square units; triangle 3 = 8 square units.

DP 144: 758

WEEKLY PUZZLERS

WP 1: All of the different pieces can be shown to have an area of 10 square units.

WP 2: Solutions will vary.

WP 3: The maximum amount earned is $149. Follow this path:

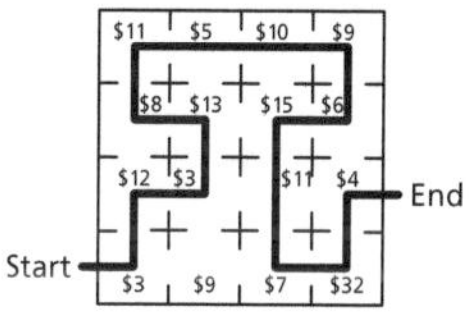

WP 4: One way to solve this problem is to set up a chart showing how the disease spreads. Starting with one infection, the disease increases this way: 1, 3, 9, 27, 81, 243, 729, 2187, 6561, 19683, 59049. Working backward seven days we find that 27 strangers came to town. If you start with 118098 people (double the population), then you can work backward seven days this way: 118098, 39366, 13122, 4374, 1458, 486, 162, 54. So 54 strangers came to town.

WP 5: The first dart will land in one of the squares. The second dart can land in the same square as the first (a miss); or in either of the squares in a different horizontal row (two misses); or in the proper square in the same horizontal row. There are four possible conditions, only one works, so the probability is $\frac{1}{4}$.

For the 3 × 3 board the first dart lands in any square. There are 8 possible conditions—two work—so the probability of the second dart landing in the right spot is $\frac{2}{8} = \frac{1}{4}$. There are now seven possible conditions, only one works, so the probability of the dart landing in the right spot is $\frac{1}{7}$. The total probability is $1 \times \frac{1}{4} \times \frac{1}{7} = \frac{1}{28}$.

WP 6: This table shows the logic:

	Pepper-mint	Choc. Mint.	Choco-late	Peach	Straw-berry
Sam	N	Y	N	N	N
Sal	N	N	Y	N	N
Sue	Y	N	N	N	N
Sri	N	N	N	Y	N
Sil	N	N	N	N	Y

WP 7: For the first ball, the heights for the bounces are 72', 36', 18', 9', 4.5', 2.25', 1.125', 0.5625'. For the second ball the heights of the bounces are 48', 16', 5.333', 1.78', 0.593', 0.198'. The bounces are never the same height.

WP 8: It isn't possible to make all three coins show heads if two coins are turned each time. It is possible to make all five coins show heads if three coins are turned each time.

WP 9: There are 60 different isosceles triangles that can be arranged into two main groups: "plain" isosceles triangles with bases of 2, 4, 6, 8, and 10—each with heights of 1 through 10; and right triangles with bases 1 through 10, each with a height the same as the number. Area for any of the triangles can be found by multiplying $\frac{1}{2} \times$ base $\times$ height.

WP 10: Put the 5 repair stations at the points that are circled.

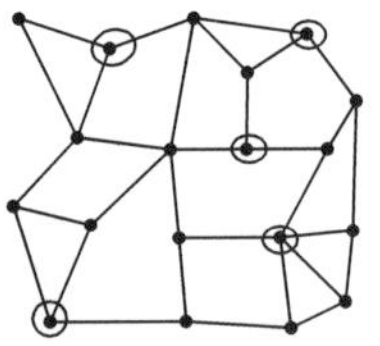

WP 11: The second player can always win. The second player should make sure that the total number of tiles removed on each turn is equal to three. If the first player takes one, the second player takes two. Now the first player can always win. The first player should remove one on his first turn. Afterwards, this player should use the same "threes" strategy as above.

WP 12: The first candidate exchanges buttons with 24 people, the second 23, the third 22, etc. The total exchanges can be expressed this way: 24 + 23 + 22 + 21 + 20 + 19 + 18 + 17 + 16 + 15 + 14 + 13 + 12 + 11 + 10 + 9 + 8 + 7 + 6 + 5 + 4 + 3 + 2 + 1 or 12 × 25 exchanges = 300 exchanges. Follow a similar process for 50 candidates = 1225 exchanges; and 100 candidates = 4950 exchanges. Formula = $n^{(n-1)/2}$

WP 13: Four boxes can be made having these dimensions: 1" × 1"x 8"= 8 cubic inches volume; 2" × 2" × 6" = 24 cubic inches volume; 3" × 3" × 4" = 36 cubic inches volume; 4" × 2" × 2" = 16 cubic inches of volume. The 3" × 3" × 4" box has the greatest volume.

WP 14: The whole number equivalents for the powers of three are: $3^1 = 3$, $3^2 = 9$, $3^3 = 27$, $3^4 = 81$, $3^5 = 243$, $3^6 = 729$, $3^7 = 2187$, $3^8 = 6561$, $3^9 = 19{,}683$. The pattern for ones digits in these numbers runs 3, 9, 7, 1. Using this pattern for 340 would involve 10 complete cycles of the pattern and the last digit would be 1. The chart for powers of five shows that after 5^1 they all end with 25, so the last two digits of 5^{100} are 25.

WP 15: Call the pineapple p; baseball b; shoe s; apple a. We know: $p + b = s$; $p = b + a$; $2s = 4a$. We can solve for p in the first equation: $p = s − b$. We can solve for a in the second equation: $a = p − b$. By substitution we see that it takes three baseballs to equal one pineapple.

WP 16: Charts will vary depending on the tires students measure. In general, it is better to have big wheels and tires because they turn more slowly when the bike is traveling at high velocity.

WP 17: One way to arrange the numbers is:

1.6	.2	.3	1.3
.5	1.1	1.0	.8
.9	.7	.6	1.2
.4	1.4	1.5	.1

WP 18: For the first two pairs, the first number is larger, after that for all such pairs the second number is larger. This is true because the larger power causes the number to be multiplied more times and this makes a greater difference than the size of the number.

WP 19: Area of square = 256 sq m. Area of shaded quarter of circle = 201.06 sq m. Area of uncovered space = 55 sq m. Rope should be 11.3 m long. (Use the Pythagorean Theorem)

WP 20: Answers will vary.

WP 21: DCBA = 13; FEBA=51; 23 = ECBA; 35 = FBA; the largest number of guests he can signal with the current system is 63. With two more lights he can signal 255 guests.

WP 22: The combinations are:

	⁻1	⁻2	⁻3	⁻4	⁻5	⁻6
1	0	⁻1	⁻2	⁻3	⁻4	⁻5
2	1	0	⁻1	⁻2	⁻3	⁻4
3	2	1	0	⁻1	⁻2	⁻3
4	3	2	1	0	⁻1	⁻2
5	4	3	2	1	0	⁻1
6	5	4	3	2	1	0

WP 23: When Lucy finishes, the coins that are in positions numbered by perfect squares (1, 4, 9, etc.) will be tails up. All of the other coins are heads up. This is due to the fact that the turning process is based on factoring the position numbers. The perfect square positions have an odd number of factors so each coin is turned over an odd number of times. Since the coins started in a heads up position, they end in a tails up position with an odd number of turns. All of the other number positions for the coins have an even number of factors so they are turned an even number of times and end in a heads up position.

WP 24: For this problem A = 1, N = 2, T = 5. Substituting gives 1.25 × 12 = 15

WP 25: Answers will vary.

WP 26: 10 dB = 10 × softest sound; 20 dB = 100 times softest sound; 30 dB = 1000 × softest sound; 40 = 10,000 × softest sound; 50 = 100,000 × softest sound; 60 = 1,000,000 × softest sound; 70 = 10,000,000 × softest sound; 80 = 100,000,000 × softest sound, 90 = 1,000,000,000 × softest sound; 100 = 10,000,000,000 × softest sound; 110 = 100,000,000,000 × softest sound. For every three steps you increase on this scale, the sound energy goes up 1,000 times.

The chart for the dB scale will be a straight line; the chart for the actual sound energies will be a steeply rising curve. You may want to discuss how the dB scale helps make these huge numbers manageable, but, at the same time, distorts them.

WP 27: Since they collected $7.25, only 29 coins were tossed. 32 = A + B + C, A + B + C − O (overlap) = 29, O = 4, so four prizes were given away.

WP 28: To analyze this game, make a table listing odd and even outcomes:

There are $^{20}/_{36}$ ways to get even sums. There are $^{16}/_{36}$ ways to get odd sums, so this game is not fair. To make it fair, replace one of the odd numbers with an even number. Outcomes will balance in number.

WP 29: To make the rectangular prism you will need: Two rectangles that are 3 cm × 2 cm and 4 rectangles that are 5 cm × 2 cm.

To make the hexahedron you will need: Six isosceles triangles with a base of 4 cm and sides that are 6 cm long.

To make the hexagonal pyramid you will need: Six isosceles triangles with a base of 10 cm and sides that are 15 cm long; 1 regular hexagon that is 10 cm on each side.

WP 30: April 5, noon; June 21, noon

WP 31: The total surface area is 24 cm² + 6 cm² + 25 cm² + 24 cm² + 6 cm² + 25 cm² + 2 cm² + 4 cm² + 16 cm² + 10 cm² + 10 cm² + 8 cm² + 8 cm² + 12 cm² = 178 cm².

The total volume = 12 cm³ + 48 cm³ + 50 cm³ = 110 cm³.

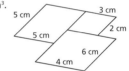

WP 32: Let s = soccer; k = basketball, a = baseball, w = swimming. We know that $s + k = 65$; $s + a = 62$; $k + w = 56$; $a + w = 53$; $a + k = 73$. By substitution we find the values $s = 27$, $k = 38$, $a = 35$, and $w = 18$.

WP 33: The other perfect number is 28. Its factors are 1, 2, 4, 7, 14, 28. If you sum the factors other than 28 you get 1 + 2 + 4 + 7 + 14 = 28.

WP 34: Examine stories to make sure they fit the data. Solutions will vary.

WP 35: This is an old, and interesting paradox. Although the sheep can be divided evenly this way, the amounts are not quite right. The oldest son is entitled to 5½ sheep, but he got 6 (½ too many). The middle son is entitled to 2¾ sheep, and he got 3 (¼ too many). The youngest son is entitled to 1⅙ sheep and he got 2 (⅚ too many). ¹/₁₂ of the original flock was not willed to anyone. This solution is probably the best if you don't want to hurt any sheep.

WP 36: One possible solution is:

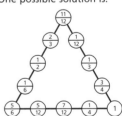

There are other solutions, too.

Daily Problems

1

What is the mystery number?

When the digits in this two-digit number are added, they give a sum that is half as large as the product of multiplying the two digits.

2

A car and a motorcycle are traveling in opposite directions at 60 miles per hour. About how far apart will they be seven minutes after they pass each other?

3

At a school carnival, students have to draw a red ball from a bag in order to win a prize. Which of the bags below gives them the best chance of winning? How do you know?

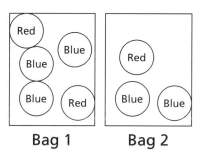

Bag 1   Bag 2

4

A worm is crawling to his home which is one meter away. The longer he crawls, the weaker he gets and the less he can crawl the next day. If he crawls within $\frac{1}{3000}$ of a meter of his home, he will find food. He must eat within twelve days. The first day he crawls $\frac{1}{2}$ meter. The second day he crawls $\frac{1}{4}$ meter. The third day he crawls $\frac{1}{8}$ meter. This pattern continues for twelve days. Make a chart that shows the distance he crawls each day, and the total distance he has covered at the end of each day. Does he make it to the food in time?

Daily Problems

5

Use an 11 × 11-pin geoboard.

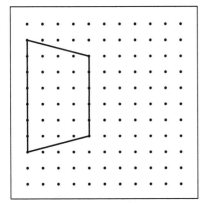 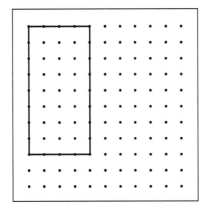 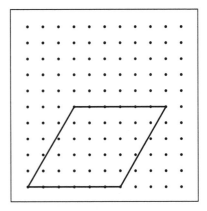

The students in Leah's class created these shapes on geoboards. Name each shape. Make a list of at least three things that these shapes have in common.

Make a different kind of shape that has the same three features in common. Sketch it on your paper.

6

Using only the number 3 and any combination of the four basic operations (+, −, ×, ÷), write equations for numbers from 1 to 10.

7

At Hula's Pizza Parlor, Jenn and her friends bought four large pizzas for a total cost of $66.10. One pizza had one topping, one had two toppings, one had three toppings, and one had four toppings. A plain pizza without toppings is $13.50. What is the price of the toppings? If each topping is the same price, what is the price of each pizza?

8

Use play coins.

Kathy is tossing two coins. What combination of coins is most likely to come up? How do you know? Draw a spinner that would produce the same probability as tossing the two coins.

Daily Problems

9

What is the mystery number? Find the smallest number that fits these clues:

It is a natural number.

It is divisible by 5 and 7.

When divided by 9, a remainder of 6 is left.

10

At Pizza Perfect these toppings are available—pepperoni, mushrooms, olives, canadian bacon, sausage, and peppers. How many different two-topping pizzas can be made? What are the choices?

11

Greenville Park has a field that is shaped like the one on the right. The people of the town want to cover it with sod to make a sports field. Sod costs $1.15 per square meter. The fund-raising committee has decided that they will invite people to "adopt" one square meter of sod. How many people need to "adopt" a square meter in order to cover the whole field?

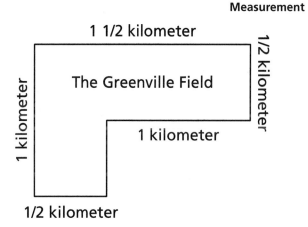

12

Phil was supposed to meet Jake early to go fishing. When Jake got up, the number of hours left in the day was three times the number of hours that had already passed. Did Jake get up early enough to go fishing?

Daily Problems

13

Use one set of pentominoes.

Look at the twelve different pentomino shapes. Do all of the pentominoes have the same area? Do they have the same perimeter? Use a chart to explain your findings. What is the difference in area between the greatest and least perimeter?

14

What is the mystery number?

Find a square number that can be made by adding together two other two-digit square numbers.

15

Use an 11×11-pin geoboard.

Use geobands to graph these two equations on the geoboard at the right. Where do the lines meet?

Equation 1: $y = 2x$

Equation 2: $y = -2x + 4$

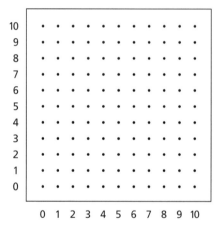

16

Jan and Dan are arguing about whether Brand X or Brand Y batteries are better. They are using the data from the table below (each square is equal to one tested battery). Find the range, the mean, and the mode for each type of battery. Use this data to prove which type of battery you think is best.

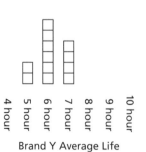

Brand X Average Life   Brand Y Average Life

Daily Problems

17

Use a protractor.

At six o'clock, the angle formed between the hands of a clock is 180°. At three o'clock, the angle formed between the hands of a clock is 90°. Make a chart. List all of the different hourly times and figure out the angle formed between the hands of the clock at each hour.

18

A train is going through a tunnel that is 650 feet long. The train is traveling 100 feet per second. The train enters the tunnel on one end. Twenty-six seconds later the last car exits the other end of the tunnel. How long is the train?

19

Find the mystery coins.

I have 99¢, but I can't give change for a half dollar, a quarter, a dime, or a nickel. What coins do I have?

20

Use color tiles.

A farmer has been growing crops very successfully. He started with two 10-acre plots. At the end of the first year, he earned enough money to buy the 10-acre plots on the border of his fences. This pattern continued year after year. How many years will it take for the farmer to own 500 acres of land?

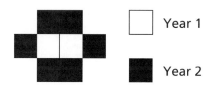

Daily Problems

21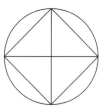

Francine took a math test. She divided by ⁻15.67 instead of multiplying by 15.67. The computation gave an answer of 25. What was the answer she should have given?

22

Geometry

The diameter of the circle is 12 centimeters. What is the area of the square?

23

Algebra

The four James children were given a gift of money from their grandmother. The oldest child got $\frac{4}{9}$ of the money. The second oldest child got $\frac{1}{3}$ of the money. The next oldest child got $\frac{1}{6}$ of the money. The youngest James child got $15. How much money did grandmother James give to the children altogether? How much did each child get?

24

Statistics

The high scorers on the girls basketball team averaged 16 points in their last game. During the game four of the girls scored: 22 points, 21 points, 15 points, and 10 points. What was the score for the fifth player?

Daily Problems

25

Draw a spinner that fits these clues:

A. The probability of spinning a 2 is equal to the probability of spinning a 1.

B. The probability of spinning all of the numbers is not equal.

C. The probability of spinning a number other than 1 is 75%.

D. There are three numbers on the spinner.

26

Use a protractor.

At three o'clock, the hour hand points directly at the three. For the seconds hand to make an angle of 72° with the hour hand, where should it be pointing?

27

The speed with which crickets chirp depends upon the temperature. Count the number of cricket chirps in a minute, divide by four and add forty to find the temperature (Farenheit). If the temperature is 84° F, how fast will crickets be chirping per minute?

28

Max discovered if he subtracted 7 from his age and multiplied by 7, he got the same answer as subtracting 9 from his age and multiplying by 9. How old is Max?

Daily Problems

29

A pair of trout are introduced into a high mountain lake. Each year the trout spawn, producing many offspring. Predators and disease kill most of the offspring, but at the end of each year, the number of trout in the lake doubles. How many years will it take for the number of trout in the lake to be greater than 2,000? Make a table and describe the patterns that you see.

30

A trader went on his rounds through the villages of his small province. In the first village, the trader spent half of his money. In the second town, the trader spent one third of what he had left. In the third town, the trader spent one fourth of what he had left. When he was done, the trader had 3 guilders. How much money did he start with?

31

Use an 11 × 11-pin geoboard.

On your geoboard make these two shapes. Now make a left-right reflection of each shape. What new shapes are produced? Give the coordinates for the all points in both figures where geobands are connected.

32

What is the mystery number?

It is larger than 100.

It is smaller than 200. It is prime.

The sum of the digits is 13.

Daily Problems

33

Rosa can count to 100 in one minute. At this rate, how long will it take her to count to a million?

34

Jill and her brother are designing a garden. They have to plan a walkway around and through the garden. They want to walk the garden without retracing any part of the path. Which of the paths will work?

Path A   Path B

35

Use an 11 × 11-pin geoboard.

Make the largest octagon you can on a geoboard. What fraction of the area of the geoboard is outside of the octagon?

36

A hot air balloon has to travel 20 miles west to land safely. It is out of fuel and cannot heat any more air. The wind is blowing to the west at five miles per hour. Every fifteen minutes, the balloon cools and loses 50 feet of altitude. If the balloon is at 835 feet, will it stay in the air long enough to land safely? Make a diagram that shows the movement of the balloon.

Daily Problems

37

In a bicycle race, Leona averages about 25 miles per hour. The race takes place between two cities 175 miles apart. How much would Leona's speed have to increase in order for her to decrease her riding time by one hour?

38

When Susan was 11, she spent about $5 on entertainment each month. When she was 13, she spent about $15 each month. If this rate of change continues, how much will she be spending when she is 15? When she is 17? Draw a line graph that shows how her spending changes each month across these years.

39

Make a chart showing how many diagonals there are for each of the shapes below. Use your chart to predict the number of diagonals for an eleven-sided figure.

40

What is the mystery number?

Add a half, a fourth, an eighth, and a sixteenth of the number together and you get 480.

Daily Problems

41

Use linking cubes.

Use 26 cubes to build the shape. Use the top-view, side-view, and front-view drawings as a guide.

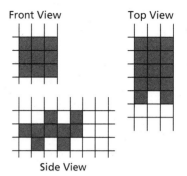

42

A bakery has been making cakes that are ten inches by twelve inches. If the bakery wants to make cakes that have four times the area, what size pans should they use?

43

A group of students is spending the day at an amusement park. They all paid the same amount for tickets. Fewer than twenty students went on the trip. The cost of the tickets was $391—everyone paid cash, using only paper money. How much were the tickets? How many students went on the trip?

44

Six kids are playing a card game at a round table like the one on the right. Use the clues to decide where each person is sitting:

1. Carly gets the first card and Phil gets the last card.

2. The dealer always gives the first card to the person on the left.

3. Laura is not sitting next to Carly.

4. Laura, who is sitting between two boys, won't sit next to Phil.

5. When Marge dropped a card, Mark picked it up with his right hand and gave it back to her without turning in his chair.

6. Todd sits between a boy and a girl.

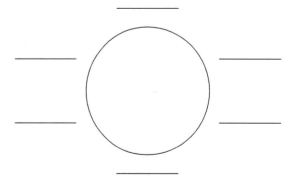

Daily Problems

45

Find the value of this expression without using a calculator:

$1.7 - 1.6 + 1.5 - 1.4 + 1.3 - 1.2 + 1.1 - 1.0 + 0.9 - 0.8 + 0.7 - 0.6 + 0.5 - 0.4 + 0.3 - 0.2 + 0.1$

46

Start with the time shown on the digital clock at the right. What time will it be in 21 digit changes?

2:47

47

The junior high basketball team has been having a great season. The team has won the last four games. The score for the first game was 72 points, the score for the second game was 64 points, the score for the third game was 86 points, and the average for all of the games was 76 points. What was the score of the fourth game?

48

Use linking cubes (two red, two green, two yellow, two blue).

Follow these clues to build a 2 × 2 cube:

The two green cubes touch on a face.

The red, yellow, and green cubes never share a face with a cube of the same color.

One red cube and one yellow cube each touch a face of a green cube.

Draw your solution.

Daily Problems

Which of these expressions have the same quotient as 25.6 ÷ 16?

A) 256 ÷ 160

B) 2.56 ÷ 1.6

C) 1.28 ÷ .8

D) 6.4 ÷ 4

E) 32,000 ÷ 20,000

---

50   Geometry

Use one set of tangrams.

There are five triangles in a set of tangrams. Examine the triangles and answer these questions:

A. Are any of the triangles congruent? If so, which ones? Explain why you believe they are congruent.

B. Are any of the triangles similar? If so, which ones? Explain why you believe they are similar.

---

51   Patterns and Functions

What are the next three numbers in this series: 4, 8, 15, 30, 37, ___, ___, ___

---

52   Probability

Arny and Frank are playing a game. They take turns tossing a coin at a calendar page that looks like the one on the right. Arny gets a point if the coin lands on a numbered square for Sunday, Monday, or Tuesday. Frank gets a point if the coin lands on a numbered square for Thursday, Friday, or Saturday. No one gets a point if the coin lands on a numbered square for Wednesday. Is this a fair game? Why or why not?

S	M	T	W	Th	F	S
		1	2	3	4	5
6	7	8	9	10	11	12
13	14	15	16	17	18	19
20	21	22	23	24	25	26
27	28	29	30	31		

Daily Problems

53

At the fabric store, there are 5 remnant pieces of cloth. They measure: $\frac{2}{7}$ yard, $\frac{4}{9}$ yard, $\frac{2}{5}$ yard, $\frac{1}{3}$ yard, and $\frac{4}{11}$ yard. The owner of the store wants the pieces folded and stacked in order with the longest on top and the smallest on the bottom. Explain how the pieces are ordered and how you reached your conclusion.

54

Moe and Joe have worked a mining claim for several years. All of the gold they found has been melted into a single brick 12 cm × 15 cm × 4 cm. Moe and Joe figure that one of them has done $\frac{2}{3}$ of the work and should get $\frac{2}{3}$ of the gold. The other has done $\frac{1}{3}$ of the work and should get $\frac{1}{3}$ of the gold. Show two different ways to divide the brick so that each miner gets his fair share.

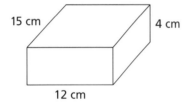

55

Use color tiles.

Nick and Jenny are playing a game. There are six tiles in a box: three red and three blue. A player picks two tiles without looking. Jenny gets a point if the tiles don't match; Nick gets a point if they do match. What are the odds that both tiles will have the same color? Is this a fair game?

56

A group of kids is riding a bus on a field trip to another town. At one point, the driver of the bus notices the number on the odometer is a palindrome—a number that reads the same forwards and backwards: 21912. How many miles will the bus go before another palindrome shows up on the odometer?

Daily Problems

Computation and Estimation

Place the operation signs + or − between the fractions below to make a true equation.

$$\frac{1}{2} \qquad \frac{1}{6} \qquad \frac{1}{8} \qquad \frac{2}{3} \qquad \frac{1}{4} \qquad \frac{4}{9} \qquad \frac{3}{8} \qquad \frac{1}{18} = 1$$

58

Logical Reasoning

Write the number 10,000 as the product of two other whole numbers. Neither of the other numbers can have a zero.

59

Patterns and Functions

Use color tiles.

Ben and Maria are making designs with color tiles. They started making the pattern on the right. Note: Only the black squares are tiles. Build the next three terms in the pattern. Then make a chart. On your chart, write down how many tiles there are in each term of the pattern. Use your chart to predict how many tiles will be in the tenth term of the series.

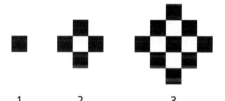

1   2   3

60

Probability

How many different ways can you arrange four books on a shelf? Explain how you got your solution.

Daily Problems

61

Place the operation signs × or ÷ between the decimals below to make a true equation.

0.1   0.5   0.6   0.12   0.2   0.25   0.5   0.1 = 1

62

Measurement

Joel is making cardboard stands for the science fair. Each stand is made from two right triangles, 12 cm × 16 cm. How many stands can Joel make out of a piece of cardboard 80 cm × 50 cm?

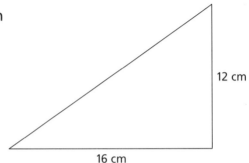

12 cm

16 cm

63

Logical Reasoning

Mike and Marcia are playing a game in the grid shown. They mark X's in the squares using different-colored markers. Every time a player marks an X, the player gets one point. The game is over if someone makes a vertical, horizontal, or diagonal row with three X's. What is the highest score a player can get in this game?

Try this game with a partner.

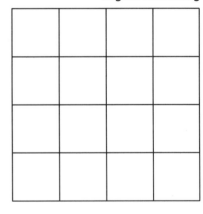

64

Statistics

Susan is on the women's fast pitch softball team. She can find her batting average by dividing the number of hits by the number of times at bat. Find her current batting average if she has made eight hits in thirty-two times at bat. Susan has one more game to go. She figures she will bat four more times in the last game. Is it possible that she will bat better than .300 for the season if she does well in the last game?

Daily Problems

Computation and estimation

Melinda says that she spent too much time driving in the car on her last family trip. Each family driver averaged 55 miles per hour. It took the family three days to drive 1650 miles. If they spent the same amount of time driving each day, how many hours were they in the car?

66

Numbers

All of the numbers in the circle are alike in two ways. Find a 1-digit and a 5-digit number that belong in the circle.

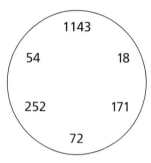

67

Logical Reasoning

Rosa is on a fishing trip with her dad and needs an empty storage box for her tackle. Her dad has his lures in 10 small storage boxes. Five boxes contain lures with or without hooks. Four contain hooks with or without lures. Three contain just lures. The rest are empty. How many are empty?

Hint: Use a Venn diagram to help you solve the problem.

68

Patterns and Functions

At the Jumping Frog contest in Calaveras County, two frogs are having a race. One frog jumps 18 cm every six seconds. The other frog jumps 7 cm every 2 seconds. Who is ahead at the end of a minute? Make an estimate. Then check your estimate using the calculator.

Daily Problems

69

The number 6 has four factors, an even number of factors. The factors are 1, 2, 3, 6. Find any numbers less than 100 that have an odd number of factors. What do you notice about these numbers?

70

Patterns and Functions

Miguel made a list of 8 numbers. Each number was three times larger than the previous number. The last number was $136\frac{11}{16}$. What were the 7 other numbers on the list?

71

Logical Reasoning

The plot of land on the right was willed to seven people. Each person wants to build a house in a different spot. Everyone wants a tree, no matter how big or small the lot is. The costs of surveying are so high, that they want to divide the property with just three boundary lines. Where will you draw the lines so that everyone gets a piece of property with a tree?

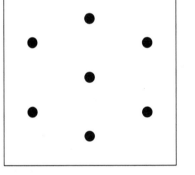

● = one tree

72

Measurement

Miguel and Luisa purchased the fish tank at the right. They plan to buy some fish for their tank, but don't know how many to get. The fish book recommends one fish per liter of water. If they fill the tank full of water, how many fish can it hold? (1 liter = 1,000 cubic centimeters)

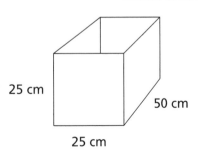

25 cm

25 cm

50 cm

Daily Problems

73

The six-digit number 67__,854 is divisible by three. What digits could go in the thousands place?

74

Statistics

June is conducting an experiment that involves measuring the growth of a plant over five days. On the first day the plant was 0.50 cm tall. On the fifth day it was 1.75 cm tall. If that the rate of growth was constant, how big was the plant on days 2, 3, and 4? Draw a line graph to show how you reached your conclusion.

75

Geometry

Use one set of tangram pieces.

Make a hexagon, using some of your tangram pieces. Sketch how you put the pieces together. How many lines of symmetry does your hexagon have?

76

Logical Reasoning

Fran, Frankie, and Flo are trying to guess the number of jelly beans in a jar. Flo guesses 132. Frankie guesses 127. Fran guesses 115. One guess is off by 12 jelly beans. One guess is off by 17 jelly beans. One guess is correct. Who was correct?

Daily Problems

77

If one side of square A measures one centimeter, what is the area and perimeter for each of the other squares? Make a chart that lists the area and perimeter of each square.

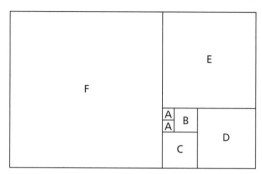

78

Use one line to divide the clock face on the right into two parts. Divide the clock face so that the sum of the numbers on one part of the face is equal to the sum of the numbers on the other part of the face.

79

The elections for President of the United States always take place on the first Tuesday after the first Monday in November. On what dates can the election take place?

80

Tim's father bought some baseball cards. He paid $8 for every six cards that he bought. Later he sold them, making a $4 profit on every three cards. If he made a profit of $24 altogether, how many cards did he buy and then sell?

Daily Problems

81

All of the numbers from 1 to 50 are written on ping pong balls and put into a box. What is the probability of drawing a prime number from the box?

82

Look at these numbers:

7, 14, 21, 35, 49, 63

Try to use these numbers to make an equation equal to 100. Use only addition and subtraction (each number may be used as many times as you wish). What did you discover?

83

The large spoked wheel turns slowly. The small disk rolls with it. The disk has a circumference of 4 cm. If the disk makes a $\frac{3}{4}$ turn between each spoke, what is the circumference of the big wheel?

84

The chart shown is a stem and leaf plot for the number of candies in 31 different boxes of SugarBursts. What is the range of the quantities of candies? What is the mode for these boxes of SugarBursts? If you had to guess how many candies would be in a box, what would you guess? Why?

Tens	Ones
1	6 6 7 7 7 8 8 8 9
2	1 1 1 2 2 3 3 3 3 3 4 4 4 4 5 5 6 6 7 8
3	3 3

Daily Problems

85

Use these digits:

6 4 2

Make as many different three-digit numbers as you can. What factors can you find for all your numbers?

86

Sam is riding in a bicycle race. Two thirds of the course runs uphill. One third runs downhill. When Sam is riding uphill, he rides at an average speed of 12 miles per hour. When he rides downhill, he rides at an average speed of 24 miles per hour. What is his average speed for the whole course?

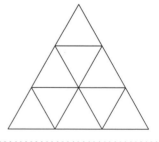

87

One of the small triangles has a perimeter of 6 inches and an area of 1.73 square inches. What is the area of the large triangle? What is the perimeter of the large triangle?

88

On the table there is a 5-liter jug full of water. There is also an empty 2-liter jug and an empty 3.5-liter jug. You can pour the water back and forth between the jugs, but you can't add any water. How can you end up with 2.5 liters in both the 5-liter and 3.5-liter jugs?

Daily Problems

89

The number 16 has five factors: 1, 2, 4, 8, 16. The number 10 has four factors: 1, 2, 5, 10. What number less than 100 has the most factors?

90

With one straight cut, you can divide a circle into two pieces at most. With two straight cuts, you can divide a circle into four pieces at most. Make a chart that shows how many pieces can be made by dividing a circle with three, four, five, and six straight cuts.

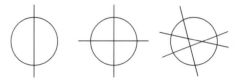

91

Eight students are sitting in the auditorium: Bart, Charles, Hank, Sam, Lucy, Mindy, Alice, and Sue. Use these clues to figure out where they are sitting:

There are two rows of four, with an equal number of males and females in each row.

No girls sit next to each other.

Alice asked Sue to remove her hat because it blocked her view.

Charles and Sam sit next to each other.

Charles won't sit next to Alice.

In the front row, boys and girls alternate their seating.

Lucy and Alice are on the ends.

Lucy could see over Bart easily because he slumped down in his chair.

92

Delia's Desserts had a special promotion one night: free samples of Extreme Chocolate, Beyond Best Chocolate Crunch, and Vanilla Extra. The black area shows the customers who tried the Extreme Chocolate, the gray area shows the people who tasted Beyond Best Chocolate Crunch, and the white area shows the fraction of people who tried Vanilla Extra. Figure out which percentage of customers tasted each kind of ice cream.

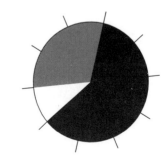

Daily Problems

93

Find the pair of mystery numbers on a number line using these clues:

One of us is positive and one of us is negative.

We are eight unit spaces apart.

One of us is three times as far from zero as the other.

94

Measurement

Vang's family is having a reunion dinner at a restaurant. There are 12 people in the family. In the restaurant, there are two sizes of round tables: 36-inch diameter and 42-inch diameter. The 36-inch diameter tables seat three, the 42-inch diameter tables seat four. The family members want to have the most space for each person. Should they sit in threes at the smaller tables or four at the larger tables?

95

Probability

There are six teams in a softball league. Each team will play each of the other teams twice. How many games will be played in this softball league?

96

Logical Reasoning

Three students—Francis, Jean, and Peg—each participate in a different sport. One plays softball. One swims. The third plays soccer. The swimmer is the youngest of the athletes. Jean is older than the softball player. The softball player's brother comes to most of her games. Francis is an only child. Match each student with a sport.

Hint: Use a diagram like this to help solve this problem.

	Softball	Swimming	Soccer
Francis			
Jean			
Peg			

Daily Problems

97
Numbers

Luisa picked two integers. She added them together, then she multiplied by 100. The answer was zero. What two integers could she have picked?

98
Probability

Draw a spinner that fits all of these clues:

A. There are five numbers on the spinner. Five is the greatest number.

B. One of the numbers on the spinner comes up about $\frac{1}{2}$ of the time.

C. The number 3 comes up about $\frac{1}{8}$ of the time.

D. The number 2 comes up most often.

E. The probabilities of 1, 4, and 5 coming up are equal.

99
Geometry

Use one set of pentominoes.

Use all 12 pentominoes to make a 6 × 10 rectangle.

100
Statistics

The graph shows the cost of clothing items at two different stores. About how much does a person save by buying clothing at the Super Discount store compared to the Value Plus store prices? Estimate the difference in percent between the two stores.

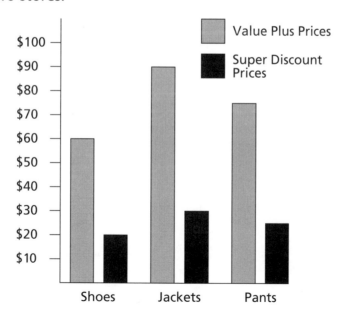

Daily Problems

101

Make a list of at least four numbers that have only three factors. What can you say about these numbers.

102

Use one set of tangrams.

If the area of tangram piece A is one square unit, what are the areas for all of the other pieces? What is the area for the whole puzzle?

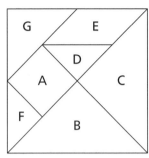

103

What are the next three numbers in this sequence:

1, 3, 6, 10, 15, _____, _____, _____

104

Ronald and Rosa are hiking. Ronald hikes four miles per hour. Rosa hikes five miles per hour. Ronald leaves camp at 8:00 AM for the trail. Rosa leaves camp at 10:00 AM for the trail. What time will it be when Rosa catches up to Ronald? Where will they be on the trail (how many miles from camp)? If they keep hiking for another two hours, how far will Rosa be ahead of Ronald?

Daily Problems and Weekly Puzzlers, Grade 7   © Ideal School Supply Company

Daily Problems

105

A six-sided cube has faces painted these colors: red, blue, yellow, orange, white, green. Study these views of the cube:

Draw the cube and show how the faces are painted.

106

Interesting patterns occur for decimal portions of quotients when numbers are divided. For instance, the chart shows the quotients for dividing numbers by 2.

As you can see from the chart, numbers divided by 2 always end with a decimal of "0" or "0.5". Investigate the other whole number divisors less than 10. Make a chart for each one. Try to find patterns for the decimal portions of their quotients.

Number being Divided	Quotient
1	0.5
2	1.0
3	1.5
4	2.0
5	2.5

107

Use toothpicks.

Rearrange six toothpicks and make a new shape with six congruent diamonds.

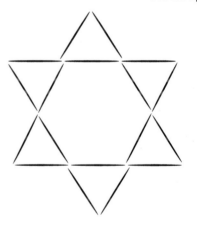

108

When an object falls, it goes faster and faster—this is called acceleration. At the end of one second, the object is traveling 32 feet per second. At the end of two seconds, it is traveling 64 feet per second. At the end of three seconds, it is traveling 96 feet per second. Find a pattern for the acceleration of a falling object. Figure out how fast the object is falling at the end of four and five seconds. Then draw a line graph showing the speeds for 1, 2, 3, 4, and 5 seconds.

Daily Problems

109

Sam is supposed to find the average length of four pieces of wood. He lays the wood end-to-end. Then he takes out his tape measure and measures their whole length. He folds this part of the tape measure in half. Then he folds it in half again. He reads off the measurement—25 inches. Does his method give the average? Why or why not?

110

The weather forecast predicts that there is a 40% chance of snow on a particular winter's day. Draw a spinner that models the probability of snow.

111

Use the following digits to fill in the boxes on the right so that you will have the smallest possible product.

3, 4, 5, 6, 7

Note: You may use each digit only once.

112

Luke has twenty bills in his wallet. He has a total of $80. If he has two more $5 bills than $10, and four more $1 bills than $5 bills, how many of each does he have?

Daily Problems

113

Use the digits below to fill in the boxes on the right so that you will have the largest possible quotient.

Digits: 5, 6, 7, 8, 9

Note: You may use each digit only once.

114

The speed of sound is about 760 miles per hour through air. The speed of sound is called "Mach." Different aircraft fly at different Mach speeds. Some jets travel at Mach 2 or Mach 3 (two or three times the speed of sound). When the Space Shuttle orbits the earth, it is traveling Mach 25. How fast is this in miles per hour? The circumference of the earth is about 25,000 miles. How long would it take the Shuttle to fly this distance?

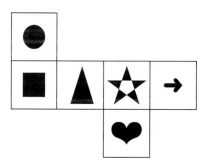

115

When the hexomino is folded into a box, which shapes will be on opposite sides?

116

Suppose you have a rich aunt who gives you one cent on your first birthday. The next year she gives you three cents, the following year, nine cents. Each year she triples the amount she gave the year before. How old will you be when you aunt gives you more than $500?

Daily Problems

117

Students in Mrs. Williams's class have been gathering data about low daytime temperature in February. The line plot below shows the data they have gathered. Find the mean and mode for this distribution.

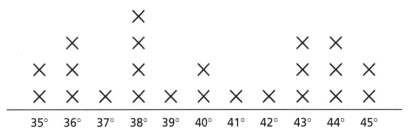

118

Use the following digits to fill in the boxes on the right so that you make an expression having the largest value possible. (The small box is for an exponent.)

Digits: 2, 3, 4

Note: You may use each digit only once.

119

In a fish tank, there are thirty-six fish. There are 24 tetras and 12 platys. The owner wants to remove all of the fish to clean the tank. The owner nets 12 fish and removes an equal number of platys and tetras. What is the probability that next fish removed will be a tetra?

120

Halley's comet was named for the English astronomer Edmond Halley, who observed it in 1682. This chunk of ice and dust orbits the sun. It is visible from the earth every 76 years. Starting with 1682, list six different years when Halley's comet has been or will be visible from the earth. Will Halley's comet be visible in your lifetime?

Daily Problems

121

The big cube on the right is made from 27 smaller cubes. Suppose all of the faces of the large cube are painted red and then it is taken apart. How many of the small cubes would have no faces painted red? One face painted red? Two faces painted red? Three faces painted red?

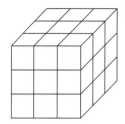

122

The number four can be written as the sum of two prime numbers (2 + 2). Test the other even numbers through thirty. See if they can all be written as the sum of two prime numbers. What did you find out?

123

The sale price chart at right was posted in Carl's Costless department store. What percent discount is being offered on these items? What is the sale price for $20 and $25? If the sale price for an item is $40, what is the regular price of the item?

Regular Price	Sale Price
$10.00	$8.00
$15.00	$12.00
$20.00	
$25.00	
$30.00	$24.00

124

Three valves control water in a pipe. All three valves are closed. Valve 1 can be opened or closed any time. Valve 2 can be opened or closed only if valve 1 is open. Valve 3 can be opened or closed only if valve 2 is open and valve 1 is closed. What is the fewest numbers of openings and closings needed to get all valves open?

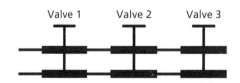

Valve 1   Valve 2   Valve 3

Daily Problems

125

In his fishing boat, Nathan went downstream moving at one hour less than he went upstream the same distance. If the current is molving at 4 miles per hour, how fast can he travel on still water, if it took him three hours to make the upstream trip?

126

The General Sherman Tree is an ancient sequoia that is about 270 feet tall. If the average seventh grader is 64 inches tall, how many seventh graders equal the height of the General Sherman Tree? Make an estimate, then use your calculator to check.

127

Use toothpicks.

Remove four toothpicks from the shape at the right and make a new shape that consists of five congruent squares.

128

What is the smallest positive integer that can be multiplied times 18 to make a perfect cube?

Daily Problems

129

Algebra

In nine years, Olga will be four times older than she is now. How old is Olga?

130

Patterns and Functions

For every turn of the big gear, the middle-sized gear turns six times. For every turn of the middle-sized gear, the little gear turns three times. If the big gear turns fifteen times, how many times does the small gear turn?

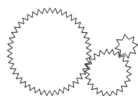

131

Measurement

Read the story below. Figure out which of the metric units belongs on the lines.

At the zoo, Simba, the elephant is quite ill. Simba is a large animal. She stands about 3 _____ tall at the shoulder and weighs about 5 _____. To prepare her medicine, the keeper uses an eye dropper to put 10 _____ of medicine in 15 _____ of water. Then she gives Simba about 20 _____ of hay to help her digest the medicine and a couple of oranges. In one orange there is a pill that weighs about 5 _____. Afterwards, Simba takes a walk around the zoo. During the walk she travels about 2 _____.

grams   milliliters   meters   kilometers   tons   liters   kilograms

132

Probability

My drawer contains black, blue, and brown socks. If I pick socks from the drawer in the dark, what is the fewest number of socks I have to pick before I can be sure I have a matched pair?

Daily Problems

133

The pizza at the right is divided into pieces that are all equal in size. Max says he wants a section of the pizza that makes an angle of 160°. How many pieces of pizza will he get? What fraction of the pizza will he eat?

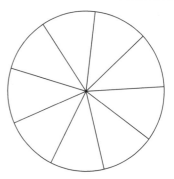

134

The amount of blood your heart pumps in one minute is called the cardiac output. Cardiac output is determined by this formula: $s \times p$ where s is the stroke volume and p is the pulse rate. The stroke volume is the amount of blood the heart squeezes out each time it beats. For a young teenager stroke volume is about 60 ml. Find your pulse. Use your pulse to figure out your cardiac output.

135

Erin's younger sister is having a birthday party. To keep the little kids occupied, Erin invents a marble drop game. The target is two square boxes, one inside of the other. The little kids can't aim very well, but they do manage to drop some marbles into the target. Will most of the marbles go into the inner box or the outer box?

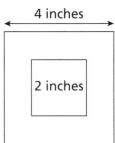

136

Aaron and Darrin went shopping. They bought the same coat at different stores. The regular price for the coat in both stores was $50. Aaron bought the coat at his store for 50% off the regular price. At his store Darrin found the coat marked with a price that was 30% off the original price. When Darrin got to the cash register, the clerk took 20% more off the marked down price. Who got the better deal?

Daily Problems

137

Lenny, a basketball star, makes 80% of his free throws. If Lenny shoots two free throws in a row, what are the chances he will sink both of them?

138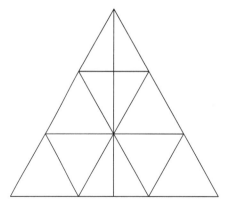

Patterns and Functions

A bus with 60 seats is coming down Main Street. At the first stop the bus picks up three passengers. At the second stop it picks up five passengers. After that, the number of passengers picked up at every stop is equal to the sum of the passengers picked up at the previous two stops. At what stop are the bus seats full?

139

Measurement

Use color tiles.

Make as many different rectangles as you can. Each rectangle must have a perimeter of sixteen. Draw each rectangle, labeling the length, width, and area. Which of your rectangles has the largest area?

140

Geometry

How many different triangles can you find in this figure? How many are equilateral triangles? How many are right triangles?

Daily Problems

141

Ten coins are in a stack. There are at least one penny, one nickel, one dime, and one quarter. There are more nickels than dimes. There are more quarters than nickels. There are more pennies than quarters. What is the probability of picking each kind of coin from the stack?

142

Look at the chart on the right. On what day did the temperature change the most from 11 A.M. to 11 P.M.? On what day did the temperature change the least? What is the average temperature for each time of day?

Day	11 A.M. Temp	11 P.M. Temp
Jan. 15	10°c	3°c
Jan. 16	7°c	⁻5°c
Jan. 17	4°c	⁻2°c
Jan. 18	10°c	0°c
Jan. 19	10°c	2°c
Jan. 20	12°c	4°c
Jan. 21	7°c	⁻1°c

143

Use an 11 × 11-pin geoboard.

Find the area of the triangles on the geoboard at the right.

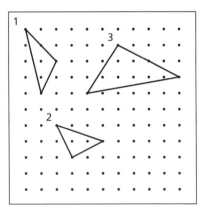

144

What is the mystery number?

This three digit number has a hundreds digit two greater than the tens digit, and a ones digit one greater than the hundreds digit. The sum of the hundreds and ones digits is three times greater than the tens digit.

Daily Problems and Weekly Puzzlers, Grade 7   © Ideal School Supply Company

Weekly Puzzlers

1

Use an 11 × 11-pin geoboard.

The rectangle on the geoboard below is divided into four pieces. Do all of the pieces have the same area? Find a way to prove your answer and be ready to share your proof with the class.

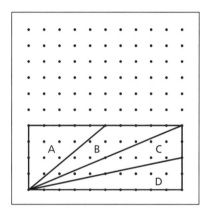

2

Look through newspapers and magazines for five days. Look for graphs and cut them out. Sort them by type: bar graph, circle graph, line graph, etc. Paste them on paper. Write a brief description of what the graphs display.

Which graphs are easy to read? Do you get a lot of information from each graph? Do any graphs distort the data? Would you change any of the graphs? How?

Weekly Puzzlers

3

Travel through the rooms in the maze shown. As you enter each room, collect the money in it. You may enter each room only once. Find the path that makes the most money.

Make up a new maze puzzle. Put new amounts of money in each square. Choose where to put Start and End. Have a friend solve your maze puzzle.

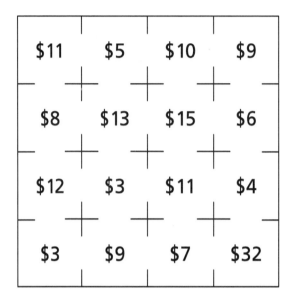

4

In the town of Kopperville, some sick strangers came to town with a bad cold virus. It seems that every time a person catches the cold, he or she spreads it to exactly 3 new people within one day. It took seven days for everyone in the town of 59,049 to catch the cold. How many sick strangers came to town? Show how you arrived at your solution.

Suppose strangers came to a town with twice the population of Kopperville. How many days would it take for everyone in that town to catch the cold? Make a prediction. Then find out if your prediction is correct.

Weekly Puzzlers

5

Ben throws two darts at dart board A pictured at the right. What is the probability that the darts will land in two different squares that are in the same horizontal row? Show how you got your answer.

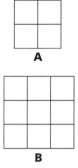

Suppose Ben uses dart board B shown at the right. What is the probability that the darts will land in three different squares that are in the same horizontal row?

6

Yummy Yogurt serves five flavors of frozen yogurt—peppermint stick, chocolate mint chip, chocolate, peach, and strawberry. Sil, Sri, Sue, Sam and Sal have each ordered a different flavor. Use the information below to match the favorite flavor of yogurt to each person:

Sam does not like yogurt with fruit flavors and neither does Sue.

Someone saw what Sal got, it was either plain chocolate or peppermint stick.

Sil is allergic to peaches.

Sue hates chocolate.

Sil will not eat yogurt with mint and neither will Sal.

Hint: Use a diagram to help you solve this problem.

Now make up your own problem. Have a friend solve your logic puzzle.

Weekly Puzzlers

7

A ball is dropped from a height of 144 feet. On each bounce it bounces $\frac{1}{2}$ the height of the previous bounce. What are the heights of the first eight bounces? A different ball is dropped from the same height. It bounces $\frac{1}{3}$ the height of the previous bounce. What are the heights of the first six bounces? Which of the bounces, if any, are the same height for the two different balls? Draw diagrams showing the bounces for each ball.

Try this with a ball. Count the number of bounces before the ball stops bouncing. Find a way to get a good estimate of the height of each bounce. What did you find out?

8

Use play coins.

Three coins are sitting on a table this way:

On each turn two coins must be flipped over. The goal is to make them all show heads. Is it possible? If so, how? If not, why not?

Suppose five coins are arranged this way:

This time three coins must be flipped over on each turn. The goal is to make them show all heads. Is it possible? If so, how? If not, why not?

Design your own experiment using four coins.

Weekly Puzzlers

9

Use an 11 × 11-pin geoboard.

How many different isosceles triangles can you make on an 11-pin geoboard? Give the base, height, and area for each one.

⋯⋯

10

The citizens of Cycleton are holding bicycle races on the downtown streets. The streets are laid out as in the map shown below. Different races will follow different streets. The organizers of the race want to be sure that help is at hand if bicycles break down. They want to set up repair stations so that help is never more than a block away from any contestant who has problems. It costs quite a bit to outfit the repair stations, so the organizers want to set up the smallest possible number. How many repair stations will they need and where should they put them?

Draw your own town map. Figure out the smallest number of stations required for your map. Have other students solve your Cycleton problem.

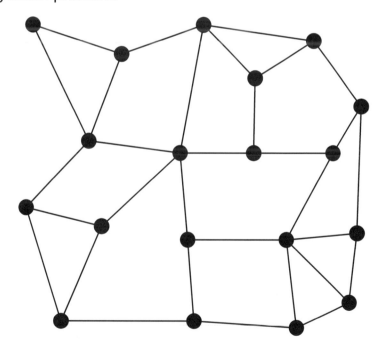

Weekly Puzzlers

11

Use color tiles.

Sue and Rhea are playing a game with 13 color tiles. On each turn a player can remove one or two tiles. The person who takes the last tile loses. Assume that Sue always goes first and Rhea always goes second. Figure out a strategy by which one of the girls can always win.

Sue and Rhea have decided to change the rules. Now the player who takes the last tile wins. Figure out a strategy by which one player can always win.

12

During a school election, all 25 of the candidates are meeting in one room. They each have campaign buttons to distribute as a part of their campaigns. In order to insure that everyone is following the election rules, all candidates need to inspect the buttons that are being distributed. On a signal, the candidates will swap buttons. Each time a pair of students meets, they swap. How many swaps will it take for all 25 candidates to trade buttons?

Suppose there are 50 candidates? Suppose there are 100 candidates?

Weekly Puzzlers

13

You can make an open box out of a sheet of paper by cutting out the corners and folding up the sides. Like this:

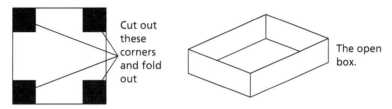

Cut out these corners and fold out

The open box.

Start with a 10 inch by 10 inch piece of newspaper or butcher paper. If measurements are always made to an inch mark, how many different boxes can you make? Which box has the greatest volume?

14

Make a chart that lists the whole number values for 3^1 to 3^9. What pattern do you see for the ones digits in these numbers? Use the pattern to predict what the last digit of 3^{40} will be.

Use what you have learned about patterns for powers to solve this problem: What are the last two digits of 5^{100}? Experiment with other power patterns.

Pose and solve your own power pattern problem. Share your problem with a partner.

Weekly Puzzlers

15

How many baseballs equal
1 pineapple?

Create your own problem.
Show four scales. Have a
friend solve your problem.

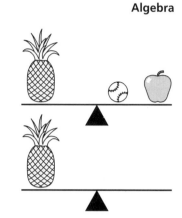

- -

16

Bicycle tires and wheels come in a variety of sizes. Measure
the diameter of several bicycle wheels from the outer
edges of the tires. Make a chart recording the diameter of
the tires. Use this information to find the circumference of
the tires.

Once you have found the circumferences of the tires,
figure out how many times each tire needs to spin in order
to travel one mile. Add this information to your chart.

Next figure out how fast the tire is spinning at fifteen miles per hour. Add this
information to your chart.

Use the information from your chart to answer this question: When traveling at
high speeds on a bicycle, is it better to have big wheels and tires or small
wheels and tires? Why?

Weekly Puzzlers

17

In a magic square, the sums of the numbers in the rows, columns and diagonals are equal. Use a 4 × 4 grid to make a magic square for these numbers: 0.1, 0.2, 0.3, 0.4, … 1.4, 1.5, 1.6. (Hint: the sum for all numbers in the magic square will be 3.4).

Make your own decimal magic square using a 4 × 4 matrix. Have other students solve your magic square puzzle.

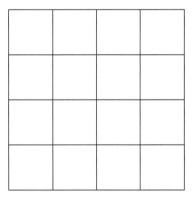

18

Look at this pair of numbers: 2^1 and 1^2. Which number is greater? Now try these pairs: 3^2 and 2^3, 4^3 and 3^4, 5^4 and 4^5. For each pair, which number is greater?

Try some pairs of your own. Write a rule that you can use to predict which number of any such pair will be greater. Explain why your rule works.

Weekly Puzzlers

19

Four goats are kept in a square pen. Each side of the pen is 16 meters long. There is a post at each corner. Each goat is tied to a different post with 8 meters of rope. The goats eat all of the grass they can reach. The white area in the center is the area they can't eat. What is the area of the grass that is left? How long should the ropes be for the goats to eat all of the grass?

Design a new goat problem. Have a friend solve your problem.

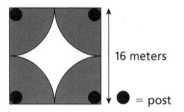

16 meters

● = post

20

When you cross a street at a traffic light, do you feel rushed, or do you feel like you have enough time to cross?

Traffic engineers spend time collecting data on how fast people walk, and how long it takes them to cross streets. They use this data to plan the length of time street lights should allow for pedestrians.

Gather data on yourself, friends, and family. Time how long it takes people to cross a two lane street at a normal walking pace. You may want to report your data according to the age of the walker.

Next, time how long traffic lights in your area allow for pedestrians to cross. Are the lights consistent or do they vary? Do the lights allow enough time for your average walker to cross the street? Does your data indicate that any of the people in your walking sample might have trouble crossing in the time the lights allow?

Share your findings with a small group or the class.

Weekly Puzzlers

21

Jose and Erica run a restaurant called The Pirate Cafe on an old ship in the middle of a bay. Each night they serve dinner to people who take a ferry out to the ship. Jake runs the ferry service and takes reservations for dinner.

The old ship doesn't have a radio or phone, so Jake uses the bank of lights on the pier to tell Jose and Erica how many people are coming. The bank of six lights is arranged in a straight line.

If light A is on, then one person is coming. If light B is on, two people are coming. If light C is on, four people are coming. This pattern continues for all of the lights. If lights A and B are on, three people are coming. If A and C are on, 5 people are coming; B and C show 6 people; A, B, and C show 7; and just D alone shows that 8 people are coming.

Suppose lights D, C, and A are on—how many people are coming? What about lights F, E, B, A? How would Jake say that 23 people are coming? What about 35 people?

Using their current system of lights, what is the largest quantity of people Jake could show? Suppose they added two more lights—what is the largest number Jake could show then?

....

22

Flo has two six-sided dice. One die has these numbers on it: 1, 2, 3, 4, 5, 6. The other die has these numbers on it: ⁻1, ⁻2, ⁻3, ⁻4, ⁻5, ⁻6. What number combinations can be rolled with these dice? What combination has the highest probability of being rolled? Could you use these dice with a regular gameboard?

Design a gameboard to use with these dice. Write the numbers on blank dice and try out the game.

Weekly Puzzlers

23

Use play coins.

Lucy has a row of one hundred coins on the table in front of her. Each coin is numbered. They are all arranged heads up. First she turns over all of the coins. Then she turns over only the even numbered coins. Then she turns over every third coin, then every fourth, fifth, etc. She does this until on her very last turn she turns over just the 100th coin. When she finishes, which coins will be heads up? Which coins will be tails up? Explain why the coins wind up in the positions they do.

24

What numbers can replace the letters in the multiplication problem shown below? Replace each letter with the same number.

Create your own letter puzzle. Use any of the operations you wish. Trade puzzles with other students in the class.

$$
\begin{array}{r}
\text{A.NT} \\
\times\ \text{AN} \\
\hline
\text{AT}
\end{array}
$$

Weekly Puzzlers

25

Choose two pages of the newspaper that have news and ads. Look at these same two pages in the paper every day for four days. Figure out how much of the area of each page is news and how much is ads. Do these areas change from day to day? On the fourth dasy, average your results. Compare your information with the information from other students. What did you find out?

26

All of the sounds a person can hear are measured on the decibel (dB) scale. The softest sounds an average person can hear are 0 dB.

Sounds with ten times as much energy are 10 dB (the gentle rustle of tree leaves are at this level). Sounds with 10 times as much energy as these are 20 dB (a whisper is a 20 dB sound). Fill in the chart:

0 dB = softest energy

10 dB = 10 times the energy of the softest sound (rustle of leaves)

20 dB = 100 times the energy of the softest sound (a whisper)

30 dB = _____ times the energy of the softest sound (a quiet street at night without cars)

40 dB = _____ times the energy of the softest sound (very soft conversation)

50 dB = _____ times the energy of the softest sound (the sound of an idling engine, ten feet away)

60 dB = _____ times the energy of the softest sound (ordinary conversation)

70 dB = _____ times the energy of the softest sound (a loud singer three feet away)

80 dB = _____ times the energy of the softest sound (city traffic as heard from inside the average car)

90 dB = _____ times the energy of the softest sound (the noise inside of a subway car)

100 dB = _____ times the energy of the softest sound (a noisy kitchen with blender, mixer, etc. going)

110 dB = _____ times the energy of the softest sound (a power mower)

Pick any two sounds on the chart. How much more powerful is the loudest than the softest? For every three steps you go up this scale, how much does the power of the sound increase?

Make two charts. On one chart, show the increase in sound as measured in dB. On the other chart, show the increase in actual sound energy.

Weekly Puzzlers

27

Use play coins.

Tania and Molly are helping their parents run the elementary school carnival. They are in charge of a quarter-toss game. Three rings are linked together like this:

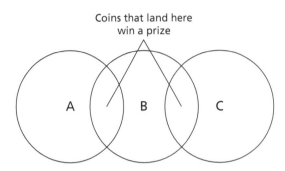

Quarters that land in the areas of overlap win prizes. At the end of the evening, Tania and Molly try to stump their parents. They say: "We earned $7.25. Thirteen coins landed in circle A. Nine coins landed in circle B. Eleven coins landed in circle C." How many prizes did they give away? Where did the coins land?

Make up your own toss game for the three circles. Make your game a dime-, quarter-, or half-dollar toss. Try out your game.

....

28

Use a spinner.

Jack and Jane are playing a game with the spinner on the right. Each person spins the spinner twice. The numbers are then added. If the sum is an odd number, Jack gets a point. If the sum is an even number, Jane gets a point. Will you get more even sums, more odd sums, or an equal number of each? Is this game fair? Why or why not? If the game is not fair, how could it be made fair?

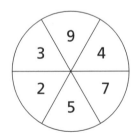

Put different numbers on the spinner. Design a new game. Make a version of the game that is unfair and a version that is fair. Try the game with a partner.

Weekly Puzzlers

29

Geometry

Use paper or cardboard, a ruler, and scissors.

You have found a set of cardboard polyhedra. You want to make a duplicate set for a friend. Here are the polyhedra:

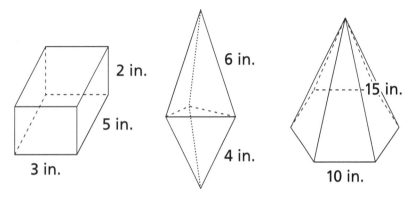

How many faces do you need? What shape and size will each face be?

Now build each of the polyhedra.

30

Patterns and Functions

At a garage sale, Ben and Gwen buy an old wind-up clock. At noon on March 1, they take it home, wind it, and set it. They discover after a few days that the clock is losing 20 minutes per day. What will be the next date when the clock shows the correct time? What time will it show?

On April 10, Ben and Gwen have the clock adjusted, but it still doesn't run correctly. Now it loses 10 minutes per day. What will be the next date when the clock shows the correct time? What time will it show?

Weekly Puzzlers

31

Find the volume and surface area of this figure:

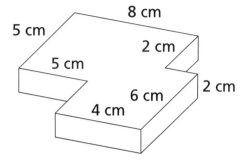

- -

32

At the junior high, there are four after-school sports programs that meet during the year: soccer, basketball, baseball, and swimming. Mr. Brown, who coaches both soccer and basketball, works with 65 students during the year. Ms. Smith, who coaches baseball and swimming, works with 53 students during the year. Mr. Franklin, who coaches both soccer and baseball works with 62 students during the year. Ms. Jefferson, who coaches both swimming and basketball, works with 56 kids during the year. Ms. Lewis, who coaches both baseball and basketball works with 73 students during the school year. How many students are enrolled in each program?

Write your own problem for these four sports. Exchange problems with another student.

Weekly Puzzlers

33

The factors of 6 are 1, 2, 3, 6. If you sum all of the factors except 6, you get 1 + 2 + 3 = 6 so the sum of the factors of 6 is equal to 6. This makes 6 a "perfect number." The number 8 has these factors: 1, 2, 4, 8. If you sum the factors other than 8 you get 1 + 2 + 3 = 7. Since the sum of the factors is not equal to 8, it is not a perfect number. There are very few perfect numbers.

Look for all the perfect numbers less than 100.

34

Every graph tells a story. For example, the graph on the right shows money in a wallet over three days. One story that could go with this graph is:

On Monday, Jill had $5. On Tuesday she baby sat for some friends and earned $15 more. On Wednesday, she bought a cd on sale for $10.

Many other stories could fit this graph as well.

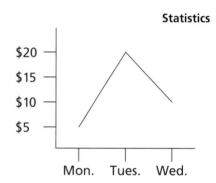

Invent a story for the graph below. The graph shows how far six people were from an ice cream stand on a busy street corner at different times one Saturday afternoon. Create any story that you wish, but you must tell what all six people were doing and your story must fit the data on the graph.

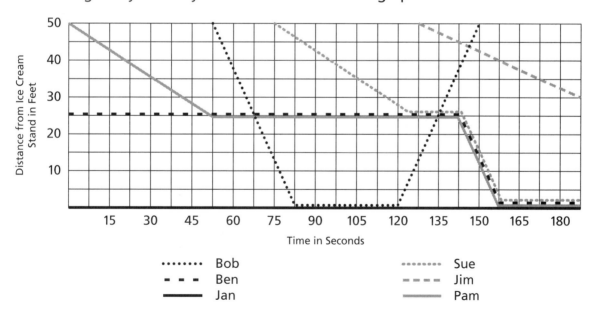

Weekly Puzzlers

35

An old farmer had three sons who helped him tend his flock of sheep which they sheared for their valuable wool. When the old farmer died, he willed the sheep to his sons. The will said that the oldest son would get half of the sheep, the middle son would get one fourth of the sheep and the youngest son would get one sixth of the sheep. Unfortunately there were eleven sheep in the flock when the farmer died and this presented some problems for the sons.

They were busy arguing about what to do, when the neighbor's daughter came along the road with her flock of sheep. "I will help you solve the problem," she said. "I will lend you one of my sheep for a few minutes. Now you have twelve sheep."

She continued, "Oldest son, you take six, which is half of the twelve sheep. Middle son, you take three which is one fourth of the twelve sheep. Youngest son, you take two which is one sixth of the twelve sheep. As you can see, there is now one sheep left over—he is mine and I will take him with me."

What to you think of the solution? Did everyone get the proper amount of sheep? Is this a good solution? Why or why not? Can you think of a better way to divide the sheep (without killing any)?

36

Fill in the circles on the triangle with these numbers: $\frac{1}{12}$, $\frac{1}{6}$, $\frac{1}{3}$, $\frac{1}{4}$, $\frac{5}{12}$, $\frac{1}{2}$, $\frac{7}{12}$, $\frac{3}{4}$, $\frac{2}{3}$, $\frac{5}{6}$, 1. Make sure that the numbers on each side of the triangle add up to $3\frac{1}{12}$. Each number can be used just once.

Draw a triangle with three circles on each side. Create your own magic triangle. Have a friend solve your puzzle.

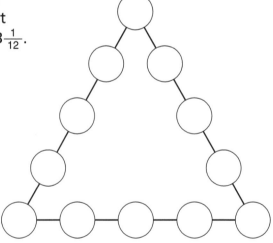